Eric's Blog Book

::

ERIC FERGUSON

Eric's Blog Book

Eric Ferguson

Ciencias Sociales y Humanas

Metanoia Missions International

Managua

ISBN 978-0-9835821-1-3

Printed in the United States of America

Cover photo by © Richard Goerg

Book design by Lorinda Gray/The Ragamuffin Acre

www.ragamuffinphotography.com

This book is dedicated to all of
Metanoia Missions International's
faithful supporters.

Thank you for believing in us
the vision that God has
placed in our hearts.

Contents

Contents

Eric's Blog Book

INTRODUCTION

After receiving several emails encouraging me to compile my blog teachings into a book format, we finally moved forward with the idea. The writings you now hold in your hand have been edited, adapted, and compiled from the Metanoia Live Blog. Many thanks to Jessica Bishop for her editing and proofing skills. May they be a blessing and encouragement to you. Blessings!

www.metanoiamissions.typepad.com

A Leader's Security

part one

■ **There** are three areas in which leaders need to be secure. The first area is personal security, which comes from a positive self-image.

As Christian leaders we must understand who we are. Our identity, self-image and self-worth, come from who we are in Christ. Our self-image should not come from our leadership position, our present job situation, our relationships, or our degrees. Our self-image must be found in Christ and Christ alone.

It's when we look at other things for our self-image that the scrutinizing gets to us. It's when we look to the ministry that we are working in for our identity that the criticizing gets to us. It's when we turn away from Christ as our security that being publicized causes us to fall. If we are not building our self-image upon Christ, we will always have a battle being waged in our minds, and I guarantee you that 99.9% of the time your insecurities will get the best of you instead of you getting the best of the situation!

Remember, Gideon was called by God to be a Mighty Warrior. However, he had to embrace who he was in God before he could go out and do anything great for the Lord. Gideon had to develop his personal security in God first, and if you remember the story, that's why he put out fleeces before God. He didn't have this first point established in his life! Once we understand who we are in Christ, we can truly move on and be effective and affective for the Kingdom of God.

A Leader's Security

part two

▓ **In addition** to the security of a positive self-image founded upon God, leaders need public security, which comes from a clear calling of God.

It is one thing to get out there and just do the work, to see a need and jump in there and serve; but it is something completely different to be called by God to a particular ministry or place of leadership. I strongly believe the saying, "Where God appoints you, He also anoints you!"

Our public security will come from our assurance that God is with us when we are leading our group, teaching a class, or evangelizing. Our public security might even come by knowing that God has called us to help build the church we attend and fulfill the vision that God has placed in the heart of our senior pastor. We need to remember the Word of the Lord that Jeremiah said, "Before I formed you in the womb I knew you, before you were born I set you apart; I appointed you as a prophet to the nations." Before we were even formed in our mother's womb, God had already picked us to be leaders.

Thus, it doesn't matter what people say, we have been chosen by God! God is calling each and every one of us to reach our cities and our countries for Him! When Satan comes along—and yes, I did say when he comes along—and starts doing battle in our minds, we need to remember who we are in Christ and what God is calling us to do!

Think back to Gideon for a moment. The Lord said to go and save Israel. He said, "You are a mighty warrior and I am sending you!" Man, if that isn't enough of a sure calling, I don't know what is! However, Gideon still didn't quite get this point at first. Gideon still had one more battle going on in his mind that he needed to conquer first.

9

A Leader's Security

part three

Leaders need a positive self-image founded upon God, public security, and thirdly...leaders need people security, which comes from being delivered from fear.

If we are going to lead people, we cannot be afraid of them. We can't be afraid of what they think. We can't be afraid of what they might say. We can't be afraid of their family name or influence. We can't be afraid because they are more gifted or talented than us. The Apostle Paul told Timothy, "God has not given us a spirit of fear, but of power, love, and a sound mind." We cannot have a sound mind if we are battling fear in our minds.

Gideon didn't think he had what it took to lead Israel. I'm sure he was quite terrified, but if he wouldn't have dealt with his fear, he wouldn't have amounted to anything. Once people understand who they are in Christ and what God has called them to do at that particular time, they can then rest assured that God will give them the wisdom and strength to lead others.

Once we lay our burdens down and cast off the spirit of fear, we can begin to move into people security. We are no longer afraid to be in front of people. We are no longer afraid to be scrutinized by those around us. We are no longer fearful of being criticized. We are no longer afraid of being publicized. We have won against the battle that was going on in our minds!

We have been working through our insecurities and now we are getting into the place where God can use us for His glory and honor. As we do these things, we can become like Gideon, who overcame his insecurities and won the battles in his mind and went on to...destroy the altar of Baal, build an altar to the Lord, have his prayers answered, lead

10

the Israelites to victory, conquer the Midianites, and be chosen to be king of Israel.

Hebrews 11:32-34 "And what shall I say? I do not have time to tell you about Gideon, Barak, Samson, Jephthah, David, Samuel and the prophets, who through faith conquered kingdoms, administered justice, and gained what was promised; who shut the mouths of lions, quenched the fury of the flames, and escaped the edge of the sword; whose weaknesses was turned to strength; and who became powerful in battle and routed foreign armies."

A Leadership Thought to Always Remember

As we all know, leadership is influence. Because a leader has influence, he or she will be out front leading the way. However, there is something that we, as Christian leaders, often overlook in our efforts to become better, more effective leaders. Many times we fail to recognize that we are Christians before we are leaders. In other words, we often put so much focus on being a leader, or on our responsibilities, position, and ministries, that we fail to focus on the fact that we are Christians—or as the word signifies, followers of Christ.

I know that I'm preaching to the choir here because I am as guilty of this as every other John Doe. We, as leaders, tend to listen to scores of teachings on leadership, devote hours a week to reading books on leadership, and even attend leadership conferences throughout the year. Now, as important as this may be, how much time do we actually focus on becoming more like Christ? I'm not asking, "How much time do we devote to becoming better Christian leaders?"...I'm asking, "How much time do we focus on developing the characteristics of Christ in our lives?" Remember, we are Christians before we are leaders.

Sure, at the time I'm writing this, I am the Senior Executive Pastor of a church with the average weekend attendance of 7,500 people, so you could say that I am a leader because I have an influence over a large group of people. However, if you take me out of this position, I may no longer have a title or position or the influence of a leader, but I will still be a Christian. Thus, regardless of how far I climb on the ladder of influence or what title I may one day carry, if you took it all away, I would still be a Christian. That, my friends, should be the foundation of our leadership.

Our leadership should be a reflection of our relationship with Christ. As important as it is to study and learn, our ability to lead should not come from a book or a class but from our relationship with Christ. If we want to be a better leader, we need to spend time in prayer. If we want to be more effective, we need to spend more time in God's Word. If we want to experience breakthroughs in our leadership, then we need to spend time fasting and seeking the face of God. It is when we get back to the basics of Christianity and focus on God and glorifying Him, as opposed to trying to reach some new level of leadership, that all the things that we heard, studied, and read regarding leadership can truly be put into practice. We need to remember that we are Christians first before everything else.

13

A Mile Wide, But an Inch Deep

Allow me to share with you one of the most popular passages in the Bible. I think that as Evangelicals, these verses are probably the second most recognized passage of Scripture…second only to John 3:16.

Matthew 28:18-20 "And Jesus came and spoke to them, saying, 'All authority has been given to Me in heaven and on earth. Go therefore and make disciples of all the nations, baptizing them in the name of the Father and of the Son and of the Holy Spirit, teaching them to observe all things that I have commanded you; and lo, I am with you always, even to the end of the age.'"

We have come to know this passage of Scripture as the "Great Commission." As Christians, these three verses of Scripture are our marching orders. Since the day that Christ spoke these words to the disciples, Christians have understood that it is their job to "go into all the world and preach the Gospel." In fact, we continually hear messages preached from this passage of Scripture; there are hundreds of books published regarding these words that Christ spoke; and people continually go to foreign countries as missionaries to fulfill this commandment of Christ.

I find it interesting though, that even with all the focus that this passage receives, the "Great Commission" is actually one of the greatest failures in the church. Sure, we do a great job sending missionaries to foreign lands. Sure, the church does a great job staying technologically advanced. Sure, many churches are staying culturally relevant. Sure, there are churches all over the world that are filling their sanctuaries every Sunday. Sure, there are new churches being planted every week. However, we have lost focus of what Jesus commanded us to do…GO AND MAKE DISCIPLES!

Without discipleship, people will never truly understand how to live a life of faith. Without discipleship, believers will never grow to their full potential and become the men and women of God that He desires them to be. It is great to see the church growing in numbers, but I would much rather see it grow in depth. There is a common phrase floating around regarding the church that I believe is true: "The church is a mile wide, but only inches deep." The Church, or Body of Christ, will not grow in depth unless we get back to fulfilling what Jesus said...GO AND MAKE DISCIPLES!

Discipleship is not about making converts. It's about mentoring, teaching, modeling, and investing one's life into the life of another. Discipleship is not easy. It takes time, energy, resources, focus, and a willingness to open your heart and allow people to see the real you. Maybe that's why there aren't a lot of people making disciples—because you have to be vulnerable. It's a lot easier to catch the fish than it is to clean them. However, Christ made it pretty clear that just catching the fish wasn't enough. Someone has to clean them. GO AND MAKE DISCIPLES. As Christians, it isn't an option; it's mandatory.

As For Me and My House

■ **Raising children** is certainly never an easy task. It seems that once you've worked through one family crisis, another one comes along. Every time you turn around someone has a word of advice for you. Friends and relatives seem to be constantly offering unsolicited advice. Books fill the shelves of bookstores giving out pearls of wisdom from a hundred different perspectives. However, sometimes it seems like we may never have the answers we need. I mean really, how do we raise our children? How are we supposed to guard our heritage? I think that in order to begin to answer these questions, we need to first consider what King Solomon said many, many years ago. Psalm 127:1 "Unless the Lord builds the house, its builders labor in vain. Unless the Lord watches over the city, the watchmen stand guard in vain."

It doesn't matter how many books we read. It doesn't matter how many conferences we attend. It doesn't matter how much advice and counsel we receive. Unless the Lord builds the house—unless the Lord is the foundation of our homes—we labor in vain. See, we can be good people who have gone to church for years. Maybe, we are even leaders in the church and in the community. Maybe, we are very religious people, but none of this means anything if the Lord is not building our home.

In order for the Lord to build our home, we have to do things with a purpose. We have to understand what our God given responsibilities are. We have to understand what our goal is as parents. We have to understand what it means to be successful parents. In fact, we need to ask ourselves these important questions: what is our goal as parents? What is our responsibility as parents? You see, successful parenthood is not that our kids grow-up to make lots of money. Successful parenthood is not that we raise sports stars and famous actors or that our children grow-up to earn titles and prestigious degrees. Successful parenthood is that our children reach their full potential in God. Successful parenthood is having children who are fully devoted to God. Our heart's cry should be the same as Joshua's when he said, "AS FOR ME AND MY HOUSE WE WILL SERVE THE LORD!"

17

Correction
part one

▨ **The heart** of a Christian leader should always remain open to correction. Often times, we think that once we have arrived at a particular level of leadership or have achieved a particular position of authority that we no longer have to be open to and or listen when people want to correct us. However, this concept is a lie of the devil. If a person has hardened his heart and is not open to receive correction that means that pride has set in, and as we know, pride is the root of all sin.

Listen to what the Word of God says about pride and proud people:

Proverbs 8:13 tells us that God HATES PRIDE and arrogance.

Proverbs 11:2 "When pride comes, then comes disgrace, but with humility comes wisdom."

Proverbs 16:18 "Pride goes before destruction, a haughty spirit before a fall."

Once we have hardened our hearts and have closed ourselves off to correction, we have allowed pride to take root. Once pride has taken root, it is just a matter of time until we fall completely. Solomon states very clearly in Proverbs that if we have a proud heart, we are destined for destruction!

David was open to receive correction. In 2 Samuel 12, the prophet Nathan comes to King David and rebukes him. The prophet uses a story to illustrate how awful David had been acting and how he was not living right. At this point, David had a very important choice to make. He could use his power and position as the king and have the prophet removed from his presence and then continue on with his life, or he could take to heart what the prophet was saying and make things right. Thankfully, for the sake of his own soul, David had an open heart and received the correction form the prophet.

However, I think that it is very important to point out that just because David repented and made things right with God, this didn't mean that there were not consequences followed his sin. Remember the law of motion. For every action there is an equal or greater reaction! In the same chapter of 2 Samuel, it is recorded that because of David's actions...the sword would never leave his house, calamity would come upon him out of his own household, his very wives would have sex in broad daylight where all Israel would see, and the son born in his adulterous affair with Bathsheba would die. Wow, how would you like to suffer through all of those consequences?

That is one of the things about being a leader...our actions and behaviors have a greater effect on people. Why? It is because we have an influence on people. That's why we need to be identified with Christ all the days of our lives. That's why we need to keep our hearts pure before the Lord. That's why we need to be open to correction. As a leader, you must remember that your actions aren't just affecting you but are affecting everyone around you and those you influence!

19

Correction
part two

▨ **Listen** to some of these sayings of Solomon:

Proverbs 6:23b "The corrections of discipline are the way to life."

Proverbs 15:10b "He who hates correction will die!"

Proverbs 12:1b "He who hates correction is stupid."

Listen to this one. As leaders, this one should really hit home!

Proverbs 10:17 "He who heeds discipline shows the way to life, but whoever ignores correction leads others astray."

If we ignore correction, we are leading all those people who are following us astray.

An interesting point to remember is that we aren't just talking about the people who are in your ministry or are under your leadership, but we are referring to the 10,000 potential people that experts say you will influence at some point in your life. Now, that's pretty scary—to think that our unwillingness to listen to the correction of others could cause us to potentially lead 10,000 people astray!

If this hasn't hit home yet, the Bible says in Matthew 12:36, Luke 16:2, Romans 14:12, Hebrews 4:13, and Romans 3:19 that we will all be held accountable for what we have done on the day we stand before God! Now, I do not know about you, but I do not want to be held accountable for leading people astray. I recognize that my responsibility as a Christian leader is to lead people to Christ—not lead them away from Him. Thus, I want to do my best to remain open to the correction of my brothers and sisters in Christ.

Today, think on this question: Is your heart open to receive correction?

20

Immune Builder Shaker

One time, I was traveling through the Houston airport and decided to buy an Immune Builder Shake from Smoothie King. When I finally made it to my gate and sat down to enjoy this yummy treat, a thought came to me: "This Immune Builder Shake is a lot like my devotions for my spiritual well-being." Please let me explain.

There are tons of places to grab something to eat in the Houston airport, but the majority of the things they offer aren't the best for our physical well-being. Therefore, I instead chose something that was full of vitamins and minerals—something that would help strengthen my body.

It is the same with our spiritual well-being. There are tons of things that we could do with our time, energy, and resources, but they are not all good for our spiritual immune system (our spirit man). We could opt for things that would be fun, entertaining, or exciting, but such choices would ultimately leave our spiritual immune system in a weak and/or vulnerable state. On the other hand, we could choose to spend time praying or reading the Word and ultimately build our spiritual immune system! It is a simple choice that you and I have to make everyday.

Do I Have Wisdom?

Proverbs 3:13 "Blessed is the man who finds wisdom, the man who gains understanding" (NIV).

Solomon said, "Blessed is the man who finds wisdom." I want to find wisdom, but how do I know if I have found it? Will there be a feeling that comes along with finding it? Will I begin to see things differently? Will my hair begin to turn gray? (If it is beard hair turning gray, then I must be growing wiser). How will I know if I have found it?

Proverbs 2:6 "For the Lord gives wisdom and from His mouth come knowledge and understanding." (NIV).

Until we come to the recognition that apart from God there is no true wisdom, we will never move into the wisdom that God desires for us to have—the wisdom that Solomon mentioned in the opening Scripture.

Job said, "The fear of the Lord—that is wisdom and to shun evil is understanding." (Job 28:28 NIV).

Proverbs 1:7 says, "The fear of the Lord is the beginning of wisdom." (NIV).

In the natural world and for the natural man, there is no supernatural wisdom. Though men can do certain things, only God is wise, and only those who are plugged into God can receive His wisdom.

Unfortunately, in our society, we claim that people are wise if they are smart, have a high IQ, make good decisions, and are well-read…but the Bible tells us differently. The Bible tells us that we are wise if we fear God, have a relationship with Him, and walk in obedience to His Word.

I guess that brings me back to my opening question: How will I know if I have found wisdom?

James 3:17 says, "But the wisdom that comes from heaven is first of all pure, then considerate, submissive, full of mercy and good fruit, impartial and sincere."

If we receive wisdom, the only true wisdom that comes from heaven or from God, then we should exhibit those characteristics mentioned by Jesus' half-brother, James.

If these characteristics are not in our lives, or at least growing and developing in our lives, then we can do like James suggests: "If we lack wisdom, we should ask God, who gives generously to all without finding fault, and it will be given to us." (James 1:5 NIV).

23

Don't Give Up!

There is a very moving story in the Gospels about a lady who had an issue of blood. Basically, she had her menstrual cycle 24-7 for 12 very long years. Could you imagine being this young woman? I'm sure that she wanted to get married, and I'm sure, like the majority of other young ladies, she wanted to one day have children as well. However, she couldn't! The culture said that she was "unclean" because she was sick, and it was also against the cultural norms for a woman to have sexual relations during her monthly cycle. Thus, what guy would marry a young lady that was sick, "unclean," and unable to have children?

The Bible tells us that this young lady went to doctor after doctor looking for a cure. However, every doctor took her money, giving her nothing in return. Day after day and year after year, she persevered, believing that one day she would find a cure. Unfortunately though, she spent all that she had and still couldn't find hope. Well, that is until one day she heard about a man named Jesus. She heard about how Jesus was going from town to town healing the sick and that he was actually coming her way.

On the day Jesus came to her town, this little, frail woman (bleeding for 12 years leaves one frail and weak) pushed and shoved her way through the crowds, just trying to get close enough to touch the hem of Jesus' garment. When she touched it, something supernatural happened...she was completely healed! After 12 years, the bleeding finally stopped! Her perseverance and faith paid off. Now, she was considered clean and available to be someone's beautiful bride!

What would have happened if this lady would have given up? What would have happened if after going to the fourth or fifth doctor should would have given up and accepted the doctor's diagnoses that there was no hope for her? Chances are that SHE WOULDN'T HAVE RECEIVED HER HEALING! She would have grown old and died in her sickness.

Instead, she chose not to accept the doctor's report and chose to keep moving forward! She chose to keep optimistic and not buy into the opinions of those around her. She kept her faith active and eyes focused on her target...her healing!

It doesn't matter what the state of our economy might be right now. It doesn't matter how bad your marriage might look right now. It doesn't matter how much debt you might be in right now. It doesn't matter how bleak things may seem. DON'T GIVE UP! Keep moving forward. Keep your eyes on God. Keep your eyes locked on the target that is set before you, and run with perseverance! Don't throw-in the towel before it is time. God has BIG PLANS for you...He has plans to bless and prosper you...He has plans to give you hope and a future... so keep pressing in and keep moving forward! The best is yet to come. Don't settle for anything less than God's best!

How Do You View God?

1. What is your picture of God?
2. What kind of person is God?
3. Who is God to you?

I **believe** that one of our biggest dangers is that we tend to recreate God into our own image of Him rather than seeing Him as He is revealed to us in the Bible. Many times we end up believing in the kind of god that we wish to believe in, while disliking and rejecting the One True God. The more I travel and talk to people and the more I read, the more I think that one of our greatest needs is to see God as He is.

The famous author and preacher Arthur W. Pink, once said, "The god who is talked about in the average pulpit, spoken of in Sunday School, mentioned in much of the religious literature of the day, and preached in most of the so-called Bible conferences, is a figment of human imagination, it is a mere invention of humanity."

The truth of the matter is that the God that many people believe in is not the same God that I read about in my Bible. If people truly come to know and understand the God of the Bible, they will soon realize that He is a loving, merciful, and faithful God who desires the best for His children. He isn't angry with you, nor does He want to strike you dead when you sin. Actually, He is quite the opposite. What He does desire is to have a close, intimate relationship with you. That's the God of the Bible!

You see, we don't need more religious activities. We don't need another church service or meeting. We need God! We need to know Him and experience Him. We need to have an encounter with GOD...the One True God of the Bible!

Churches around the world need to be careful because they can get people to come to their churches because things are happening. They have this activity and that activity. They have this guest speaker and that guest speaker. They have radio programs and they have television programs. Some of them have beautiful buildings. Others have great music. However, all of this is nothing if people are not experiencing God and coming to a place where they understand who He is. People need to know God!

27

It's a Matter
of the Heart

▧ **Solomon** said in Proverbs 4:23, "Above all else, guard your heart, for it is the wellspring of life."

What is he saying?

Watch your heart. Monitor your heart. Guard your heart. Take good care of it because life flows out of your heart. Life comes from our hearts. In other words, we live from our hearts. We love from our hearts. We parent from our hearts. We lead from our hearts. We manage from our hearts. We communicate from our hearts. Everything we do, the words that we say, the attitudes that we have—it all comes from our hearts. That is why Solomon said, "GUARD YOUR HEART!" Guard here means to be careful of what enters. Basically, Solomon was advising us to station a watchman at the entrance of our hearts, and make sure that we don't allow yuck to enter into our hearts.

Watch closely, and don't permit certain things to enter your heart. Remember to "guard your heart because it is the wellspring of life."

Here are a few questions we need to ask ourselves regarding this issue:

1. What are we allowing into our hearts?
2. What are our hearts full of?
3. What is our filter, keeping us from saying certain words and doing certain actions?

God is in Control
part one

I know that there are times that it doesn't seem like it, but God is in control. He always has been and always will be.

Psalm 103:19 says that "the Lord has established His throne in heaven, and His Kingdom rules over all."

I have encountered numerous people who really have a hard time believing this statement to be true. They want to have that this type of confidence, but because of their given circumstances, it is just too hard to believe it is so.

Some have said, "If God is in control of everything, then why did He allow the things that happened to me as a child to happen?"

Others say, "If God is in control, why didn't He heal my mother of cancer?"

And I've heard others say, "If God is in control, why is there so much killing in places like Africa?"

To be completely honest with you, I don't have the answers to these questions. Nor do I have the answers to the hundreds of other questions regarding God's sovereignty. However, what I do know is what the Word of God says.

Psalm 22:28 "For dominion belongs to the Lord and He rules over the nations."

Daniel 4:17 "The decision is announced by the messengers, the holy ones declare the verdict, so that the living may know that the Most High is Sovereign over the kingdoms of men and gives them to anyone He wished and sets over them the lowliest of men."

29

God is in Control
part two

■ **The interesting** thing as Christians is that so many times we struggle with trusting that God is in control for the day to day things in our lives. We often have difficulties believing God is in control in the "here and now." Although, we have 100 percent confidence that He is in control with our eternal lives. Sure, we have faith and confidence in God and His Word when we are promised to have eternal life with Him in heaven, but the problem is that we have difficulties believing that He is in control of our lives at this present moment.

Why? It is because we see our monthly house payment. We know how much our credit card bills are. We just got the test results back and know that we have cancer. We just received this month's electric bill and know we do not have the means to pay it. We know that our present income can't keep up with the inflation rate. We found out that our son is an alcoholic and our daughter is strung-out on drugs. We've just discovered that one of our employees has been stealing from us. We received news from the doctors that our new baby has a rare disease.

Sure, we have faith. Sure, we believe in God. Sure, we believe that through Christ we can have eternal life in heaven…but we really struggle with believing that He is still in control of everything in our lives between birth and death.

It's time we take a stand. We either believe the Word of God and its promises or we don't. We need to be like David who said on numerous occasions, "TRUST IN THE LORD AT ALL TIMES!" God is Omnipresent, He is Sovereign, and He is unchanging. Just like God was in control in the Old Testament, He was in control in the New Testament. Even closer to home, just like He was in control during the New Testament times, He is in control in our time! David said in Psalm 102:27, "But you remain the same, and your years will never end."

If we can believe God for our eternal salvation, how much more should we believe Him with the here and now? "Trust in the Lord at all times!" He is still on the throne and is still in control!

God is With Us and is Active in Our Lives
part one

No matter what happens in our lives, what trials and challenges we may come up against, we cannot forget God's promises. He said that He will never leave us nor forsake us! He is always here with us. As Christians, at the moment we asked Jesus to come into our lives and asked for forgiveness of our sins, the Holy Spirit came to live inside of us. Thus, we must remember that God is not only with us, but He is active in our lives.

There are entirely too many people that believe that God just sits up in heaven looking down here at the earth and watching everything happening to us. It's as if God were sitting in some big movie theater, with His feet propped-up on the seat in front of Him, eating popcorn, and watching our lives as if He were watching some movie. Wow! Image what type of movie that would be! Drama, action, suspense, violence, love, etc. It would have it all! However, that is not the way that the Bible describes our God.

The Bible tells us that God is not only with us but is active in our lives.

Psalms 34:7 "The angel of the Lord encamps around those who fear him and he delivers them."

Psalms 18:16 "He reached down from on high and took hold of me; he drew me out of deep waters."

1 Samuel 3 The Lord speaks to young Samuel in the house of Eli.

The Lord was with David and gave him strength to fight the lion, the bear, and Goliath. The Lord was with Daniel when he was thrown into the Lion's Den.

Daniel 3:22 "The kings command was so urgent and the furnace so hot that the flames of the fire killed the soldiers who took up Shadrach,

Meshach, and Abednego, and these three men, firmly tied, fell into the blazing furnace. Then King Nebuchadnezzar leaped to his feet in amazement and asked his advisers, 'Weren't there three men that we tied up and threw into the fire?' They replied, 'Certainly, O King.' He said, 'Look! I see four men walking around in the fire, unbound and unharmed, and the fourth looks like a son of the gods.'"

In Acts 12, the Angel comes and unties Peter and helps him walk out of prison. Jesus says in Matthew 28:20, "And surely I am with you always, even to the very end of the age." It should give us peace to know that God is with us and working on our behalf. It's like the psalmist wrote, "Even though I walk through the valley of the shadow of death, you are with me, your rod and your staff comfort me." No matter what size of trial we are going through, God is right there with us. Though He is not only with us, He is actually working on our behalf. If you are reading this today and you feel all alone in the battle you are in, I assure you, if you have asked Jesus into your heart as your Lord and Savior, then He is there with you. In fact, He is working on your behalf!

God Is With Us and Is Active In Our Lives

part two

I've given you Scriptures that display God's constant presence and activity in our lives, but I'd also like to share a personal experience with you.

In the summer of 1995, I drove from Texas to Pennsylvania to spend the summer with my parents. The moment I pulled into my parent's driveway, my car died. As a result, I had to borrow a car from my parents or grandmother for entire summer. It was very inconvenient, especially considering I would be getting married sometime in the near future. I prayed and prayed and prayed for a car, but I just wasn't hearing anything from God and I couldn't find anything I could afford. I battled with the thought of how God could do this, and it just didn't seem fair. Here I was in Bible college, studying to be a minister and interning at a church, so I was making basically next to nothing. However, on the last day of the internship at the church, someone took me to a car lot and bought me a brand new car.

Here I was trying to figure out why God would allow this to happen to my old car, and if nothing would have happened to my old car, then this person wouldn't have bought me a new car. You see, God had a plan and purpose in the whole process that took place. Even during our trial and battles, God has a plan and purpose for everything.

Proclaim what Jeremiah the Prophet proclaimed in Jeremiah 20:11 "THE LORD IS WITH ME LIKE A MIGHTY WARRIOR!" God is A MIGHTY WARRIOR AND HE IS WORKING ON OUR BEHALF!

So...don't give up. Don't get discouraged. Don't let the battle get the best of you. Let's consider idea number 2. It should help give us peace during our trials to know that WE ARE BEING MATURED.

Faith, Trust, and the Impossible

Faith is one of the most written about subjects in the Bible. In fact, there are 667 direct references to faith in the Bible. That's 193 in the OT and 474 in the NT. Jesus Himself referred to faith 156 times, and Paul talked about faith 192 times. Thus, as we can see, faith is a very important subject for us as believers.

Wendell Smith wrote, "Faith just doesn't believe in God, even demons do that. Faith does not just believe that the Bible is true, for even the devil recognizes that. FAITH CHANGES THE NATURAL ORDER OF THINGS. Faith generates a force, a power, and an influence, that makes changes in the natural realm through the power of the supernatural. Faith is a confident trust in the Power of the Almighty God through Jesus Christ. We don't just believe in Him, we PUT OUR TRUST IN HIM!"

I like what Pastor Smith said there: "We don't just believe in Him, but we put our trust in Him!" The truth is, and Jesus said it in Matthew 17:20, that if we put our trust in Him and have the faith to believe that He will move on our behalf, then "We can say to this mountain move from here to there and it will...nothing will be impossible for you!" Con Dios lo imposible no existe. (With God the impossible does not exist!)

What are you believing in today? Where do you place your trust? Where is your faith?

35

Leading from a Pure Heart
part one

■ **A Christian** leader's heart must be and remain pure. Notice that I specifically stated that a Christian leader's heart must be and REMAIN pure. When we start in leadership, the majority of us start with a pure heart. We usually get involved in the leadership of the church because we truly want to help people and see the world won for Jesus Christ. What happens is that after time passes and we've been through the fire a couple of times, our hearts begin to change. Maybe we've been let down one too many times, and our hearts have been affected. On the other hand, maybe we've had great success in the ministry, and it has affected our heart and motives.

That is why it is so important for us to guard our hearts and focus on our identity in Christ.

Let's consider what Paul wrote to Timothy.

According to this passage of Scripture, we have a choice as to what kind of vessel we will be. We can either be vessels of honor or vessels of dishonor. God is looking for vessels of honor. God is looking for hearts that are clean and pure. As Paul says, God is looking for "vessels for honor, sanctified, useful to the Master, prepared for every good work."

When we, as Christians, make the decision to keep our hearts pure and live according to God's Word, Paul says that WE WILL BECOME "VESSELS FOR HONOR, SANCTIFIED, and USEFUL TO THE MASTER." I love the fact that Paul uses the word sanctified because something sanctified paints such a vivid picture for me. The word sanctified means to be set apart! Paul is telling us here in 2 Timothy that if we make the choice to keep a pure heart, we will then be sanctified unto the Lord and will be prepared for every good work.

Consider this illustration I once heard:

The highest-ranking officer in the military has a military jeep wherever he is stationed in the world. No matter where he is, what time of day it is, or what is going on—this high-ranking officer always has access to this jeep and its driver. If a lower ranking officer came and tried to use this high-ranking officer's jeep and driver, he would be in BIG TROUBLE. Why? It is because this jeep has been sanctified for the high-ranking officer. This jeep and driver have been set apart for one purpose: to serve the high ranking officer!

When our hearts are pure before the Lord, we too are set-apart for a very high-ranking officer: the King of Kings and the Lord of Lords. The Christian leader who has a pure heart has been set-apart (sanctified) for the Lord. Because this leader has been set-apart, he is a powerful tool in the hand of God and will make an incredible impact on the world around him.

Leading from a Pure Heart
part two

■ **David** was one of those people who had a pure heart and was sanctified for the work of the Lord. When the prophet Samuel came to Jesse to anoint one of his sons to become the future king, Samuel choose the least likely of the eight boys.

He chose the little teenage boy named David. Why?

1 Samuel 16:7 has the answer for us. "But the Lord said to Samuel, 'Do not consider his appearance or his height, for I have rejected him. The Lord does not look at the things that man looks at. Man looks at the outward appearance, but the Lord looks at the heart.'"

The Lord chose this little shepherd boy to be the future king because he had a pure heart.

It wasn't because he was talented.

It wasn't because he was a natural-born leader.

It wasn't because he had a great education.

God chose him because he had a pure heart. In fact, the Bible even says in 1 Samuel 13:14, referring to David taking the place of Saul as king, that "the Lord has sought out a man after his own heart." Because of David's pure heart, God used him mightily. However, even though David's heart was pure and even though the Lord chose David because his heart was bent toward God, David fell. Yes, David led nations and armies, yet there was a time when his heart wasn't pure—when he fell into sin with Bathsheba. This man had so much going for him, this man was so hungry for the things of God, this man was literally selected to be king because of his pure heart, and this same man fell and fell hard!

Let's face it: there are times that we are going to really mess up. There are times that we might even fall flat on our faces.

That's exactly what happened to King David. His heart slowly drifted away from God, and he began to loose his identity in God. However, praise God that David listened to Nathan the prophet and got his act together. In fact, in Psalm 51 we can see how David humbled himself and made is heart right before the Lord.

David cries out the Lord in verses 1 and 2: "Have mercy on me, O God, according to your unfailing love; according to your great compassion blot out my transgressions. Wash away all my iniquity and cleanse me from my sin."

Then, note verse 10: "Create in me a pure heart, O God, and renew a steadfast spirit within me."

39

David truly was a man of God. He truly wanted to do what was right, and because he humbled himself before the Lord, God continued to use him for his glory and honor. As Christian leaders, we must all recognize that we are all vulnerable and have the natural born tendencies to be drawn away from God. This is why we must continually check the condition of our hearts. It's also extremely important as Christian leaders to continually apply 1 John 1:9 to our lives.

1 John 1:9 "If we confess our sins, He is faithful and just to forgive us our sins and purify us from all unrighteousness."

If you've messed up, ask for forgiveness. If you have an issue or stronghold in your life, confess it, ask for help, and let Jesus come in and touch your heart. We can't be afraid of what people will think. We can't be afraid of being embarrassed. We need to do what it takes to get our hearts right before God! The most important thing is the condition of each and every one of our hearts before God.

I want to close with two questions:

1. Are you a vessel of honor, sanctified unto the Lord?

2. Is your heart as pure as it was when you began to serve as a leader?

"No, Mom, it's not a real tattoo!"

Lately, I have had a few conversations, with people that I respect I might add, that have disturbed me. There is this notion among many Christians that because they are Christians and are saved by grace that they can do as they please for the most part. There is this idea that as long as they "love" Jesus everything else is rather irrelevant. During these conversations, I heard numerous times that the "older" Christians just need to stop being legalistic and be delivered from their "religious spirit."

Why were such comments made? It is because many "younger generation" Christians listen to a different style of praise and worship than their parents do; they do not sport a coat and tie in church; and they are into body piercing and tattoos. I'd like to add here that this isn't just a trend with the "younger generation of Christians," for I know of many ministers that fit in this category, as well.

Now, please do not get me wrong. There's not necessarily anything wrong with listening to a different style of praise and worship, ditching the coat and tie, and getting a few "I LOVE MOM" tattoos. However, the thing that I find disturbing is the attitude that the younger generation of Christians has toward the older generations. They themselves are developing the exact same spirit that they are so much against—A RELIGIOUS SPIRIT.

This younger generation of Christians does not want to worship in the same manner as their parents and grandparents; they certainly do not want to wear the clothes their parents wore to church (remember your Sunday best?); and they certainly do not want to hear anything against body piercing and tattoos. The problem is, though, and this is what I find disturbing, that if you do not do the things the way they think

40

it should be done or if you think in a manner a little different than them (old school), you are considered legalistic or have a religious spirit.

Hmmm, if they aren't accepting the older generation of Christians because their style of worship is different, and they tend to dress a little more conservative and claim that Leviticus 19:28 still holds true today, then who is being legalistic and who has a religious spirit? The one who is a little hesitant to change because they are set-in-their-ways or the one that thinks their "new" way is the right way and won't accept the older way of doing things? Now, of course I could be totally missing it here, but it seems to me like both groups are struggling with the same issue. Our way is the right way = religious spirit!

Look, I am part of the younger generation of Christians—even though my wife keeps telling me we aren't as young as I think we are—and I am afraid that many of us "young 'uns" are missing out on an inheritance of wisdom and knowledge that the older generation of Christians has to offer us because we are too stubborn and "in love with Jesus" to accept it and receive it. We'd rather keep doing our own thing, in our own way—thus putting even a greater chasm between our generations. Instead, we should embrace the best of both worlds and find a way to grow together and encourage one another.

Remember, we are all in this together. It's not about us (young guns) verses them (older generation). It's about sons finding spiritual fathers, and fathers investing in the lives of spiritual sons. However, these relationships will never exist if both generations continue to allow those religious spirits to cause division and strife in the Body of Christ.

Our Security

■ **Luke 5:4** "When he had finished speaking, he said to Simon, 'Put out into the deep water, and let down the nets.'"

Jesus told Simon Peter to "put out into the deep water," or to literally launch out into the deep. Peter couldn't catch anything sitting on the shore in his boat. If he wanted to catch fish—if he wanted to discover what was deep within the water—he had to launch out from the shore.

What is the significance of launching out? It means that Peter was going to have to leave the security and comfort of the shallow, calm water and head out into the deep sea. God wants each and every one of us to go deeper with Him. He wants us to depart from where we are and come into Him. However, in order to do so, we need to leave the security of the shallow water behind us and launch out into the deep.

Out in the deep is where all the adventure is. Out in the deep is where all the great discoveries and experiences are. However, if we don't launch out, we will never get to experience those things that God has for those out there. God made us the way He did so that He can launch us out into the deep. God wants to launch us out into the deep, so we can receive everything that He has for us on this side of heaven. We don't have to wait until heaven to receive His blessings. We can receive them now, IF WE ARE WILLING TO LAUNCH OUT AND LEAVE OUR SECURITIES BEHIND!

If we want to experience deeper things in God, sometimes we need to launch out from the security we have in this world. Often times, we get so tied to things that we can't launch out. We are like a boat that was built to cruise out in the deep ocean, but we are continually bound to the dock. We need to let go of those things that keep us tied-down and launch out into the deep.

Jesus lived to challenge man's security. Whether it was challenging people to leave their wealth behind in order to commit to Him, whether it was telling people that they needed to love Him more than their families, or whether it was telling people to literally leave everything behind and follow Him...He lived to challenge people's security.

For each and every one of us it is something different; however, that security, whatever it may be, has the potential to keep us bound to the dock and unable to launch out. Jesus is telling each and every one of us to let go of our securities and go deeper in Him. We all need to learn to let go and trust God. HE IS OUR SECURITY!

Is your security keeping you from launching out into what God wants for your life?

The Potential
of the New Year

I remember years ago, when I was a young boy, my father told me that as you grow older, the years pass by faster and faster. Wow, was he ever right! Every year seems to go by quicker than the previous year. I think that is one of the reasons that at the end of each year it is important to take time to reflect on the previous year—the year that is ending—and to make plans for the year that is ahead. It is important for each one of us to ponder the plans and goals that we set for ourselves in the beginning of this year that is ending and see where we are now.

44

How well did we do?

Did we succeed in the things that we set out to do?

Did we accomplish what we wanted to accomplish?

One of the nice things about a new year is that it offers us the chance to wipe the slate clean and start over once again. Sure, we can't take back the things that we did this past year, and we can't make up the time that we lost or wasted. However, entering into a new year does give us the opportunity to set new goals and to make new plans!

As every day in the Lord should be, I believe that this coming year is a time of new beginnings!

This is a year full of potential. It is...

potentially a year full of new opportunities!

potentially a year of a healthier-happier marriage!

potentially a year of exciting involvement in the church!

potentially a year for miracles and breakthroughs!

potentially a year of blessings!

The list of "potentials" for this year is endless!

The Vision for the New Year

■ **Knowing** that the potential for this new year is endless, I have a question for each of us: What will we do to make the "potentials" of the new year become the "reality" of the year? What kind of goals and plans are you making that will help you to become the person you want to be and accomplish the things that you desire to accomplish?

Solomon, who was the wisest person to ever live with the exception of Jesus Christ, tells us in Proverbs 29:18 that "where there is no revelation, the people cast off restraint; but blessed is he who keeps the law."

Without a vision and purpose in our lives, we will cast off all restraint and just be tossed to and fro. In many ways, this year will be what we make it to be. Thus, if you want to have a successful year, you must have a vision. If you want to be productive, it is important to develop a vision. If you want to be an effective person wherever you are in life, you must have a vision.

Author Norland Bushnell said, "Everyone gets into the shower and has an idea or vision, but the successful ones get out of the shower, dry off, and do something about it."

Vision is everything.
Vision is utterly indispensable.
Vision paints a target for us.
Vision sparks a fire within us.
Vision serves to fuel the flames in order to keep the fire going.
Vision is the driving force that keeps us moving forward.

Here's the bottom line. We can let this year pass us on by like so many other years, or we can purpose in our hearts to see this year be a year of victory, fulfilled dreams, and breakthroughs!

With that said, what will this year look like for you? What kind of plans are you making to experience fulfillment and growth in your life? I want to encourage you to think about these things, talk about them with your family, and then, come up with a game-plan for this new year of potential!

I assure you, you won't regret it.

Taking Jesus at His Word

In John 4, we find a story of a royal official whose son was close to death, so he went to Jesus and begged Him to go to his house and heal his son. However, Jesus tells the man to go home because his son had been healed. Here's the interesting point: in verse 50 the text says that "he took Jesus at His word and departed." This royal official, who was not a follower of Christ, took Jesus at His word and departed. Let me say this again. An unbeliever received Jesus' word as truth and went home, believing that his son was healed.

How many of us take Jesus at His word? How many of us accept the Word of God as the truth and go in faith believing it to be so? Unfortunately, a lot of us know what the Word says, but we don't always take it as the truth for our lives and/or circumstances. However, there are 7,874 promises given to man in the Bible, and when God makes a promise, history shows us that His promises always come to pass. Let's start taking God at His Word, and let's start believing that what He says is true and will come to pass in our lives.

Let's follow the royal official's example and see what God will do in and through our lives!

The Issue of Sin

Why is it that we've come to the place where we are afraid to address the issue of sin? Why is it that a person could turn on the television and listen to numerous preachers but never hear a thing about sin or our fallen nature? I think a good indicator of where we are in society is the fact that many Christian educators and ministers will not even address sin because of their fear of offending someone.

Please understand that I am not saying that we need to all go to the nearest street corner and begin yelling at the people passing by: "REPENT! REPENT!" However, I do think that we need to care more about people's souls and where they will spend eternity...and less of what they might think of us.

All throughout the Bible, sin is addressed. Peter said, "Repent and be baptized for the forgiveness of your sins." Jesus said, "Take heart, your sins are forgiven." John the Baptist came preaching a baptism of repentance for the forgiveness of sins. James said, "Wash your hands, you sinners, and purify your hearts, you double-minded." Moses said, "Each is to die for his own sins." Ezekiel said, "The wicked man will die for his sins."

However, in many of our churches today, we rarely hear the word sin or sinner. Yes, Jesus lectured about money. He gave instructions about the family. He taught on prayer. He spoke on fasting. He preached an awesome message on faith. Most importantly, however, He spoke about SIN!

Sure, we can lay hands on the sick and see them made well. We can pray for the blind and they will receive sight. We can pray that God will raise the dead, and they will be restored back to life. We can give all we own to the poor so that they will lack nothing, but if we never address the issue of sin, what good is it? People will be blessed, touched, prosperous, and healed but will still be headed straight to hell. I don't know about

48

you, but I don't want to see the people that I am close to die, go to hell, and suffer an eternity in agony. Instead, I want to see them in heaven, walking on streets of gold, living in mansions, and most importantly, having eternal fellowship with the King of Kings and the Lord of Lords!

It's time that the topic of sin is no longer taboo in our society.

The Iceberg
part one

▓ **In our** minds, we often think of leadership in terms of the visible—in terms of what we can actually see with our eyes. For example, we think of:

Speaking in public
Sitting on stage
Being able to draw large crowds
Being seen on television
Having a nice, big office with a nameplate on the door

However, the truth is that leadership is actually like what John Maxwell refers to as an "iceberg." Why? Because when you see an iceberg, you are only actually seeing a small fraction of the actual iceberg. The majority of its size is below the surface of the water, where the majority of people will never see it. It is the exactly the same way in leadership. The majority of things done in leadership will never be seen with our eyes.

For example, these aspects of leadership are unseen: the personal price paid by leaders (financially, mentally, physically, and with the family), the preparation required (spiritually, mentally, and emotionally), the prayers which were prayed, and the time spent dreaming/envisioning/contemplating.

The Iceberg
part two

▨ **Knowing** that the majority of leadership is unseen, let's consider one aspect of a leader's invisible life—PRAYER. A Christian leader cannot lead effectively without a prayer life. These keys must be remembered:

1. A Christian leader cannot lead people if he won't pray for them.
2. A leader leads in prayer long before he leads in public.
3. A leader's commitment to pray precedes the people's commitment to follow.
4. A leader's public prayer life is just a reflection of his personal prayer life.

In fact, a leader's prayer can tell a lot about the leader. Prayer reveals:

1. about which the leader cares
2. about which the leader is concerned
3. to what the leader is committed
4. the leader's convictions
5. what consumes the leader's life

If you have the opportunity to listen to a leader's prayer, you will know what they are about because our prayers are the reflection of our heart. Thus, a leader's prayer shows the leader's heart.

Let's consider how Jesus prayed for His disciples and see how we can follow His example.

John 17: 9-26

1. Jesus prayed for His follower's faith (v. 11-12).
2. Jesus prayed for their fulfillment (v. 13).
2. Jesus prayed for their future (v. 14-15).
2. Jesus prayed for their faithfulness (v. 16-17).
2. Jesus prayed for their fellowship (v. 25-26).
2. Jesus prayed that they would understand God's love (v. 25-26).

51

God's Purpose for You
part one

■ **Let's** be honest here, you did not choose to be born. It was way beyond your control. It was not something that you desired; it was one of those things in life that happened that you had absolutely nothing to do with. HOWEVER, GOD PLANNED IT!

It doesn't matter if you didn't like your parents, if you had a hard childhood, or even if you were given up for adoption or abandoned in the street. GOD STILL PLANNED FOR YOU TO BE BORN . . . BECAUSE HE HAD A PURPOSE IN IT. Long before your parents produced you, God had already decided for you to be born. The very fact that you are alive today is because God has a purpose for you life. THAT PURPOSE IS TO KNOW HIM!

Look back at Ephesians 1:5 in the NVI version of the Bible and circle the word "In."

God takes pleasure in us. Can you believe it? God takes pleasure in us! Why? It is because we are His creation. He made us to know Him and to love Him! EACH ONE OF US IS LITERALLY THE OBJECT OF GOD'S LOVE. You were made to be loved by God. Sure, there may be times that we disappoint God, but His love is unconditional. His love does not change based on our behavior.

God's Purpose for You
part two

Previously, we discussed how God's love for us does not change based on our behavior I'd like to illustrate this point. My wife Shanna and I love our three children. They are great, and we would do absolutely anything for them. Sure, there may be times that we allow their attitudes and behaviors to affect us. There are times that they blatantly disobey us, and we get upset and even angry sometimes. However, our love for them does not change. They are still our children, whom we love and love to love. We look forward to watching them grow and develop. We enjoy taking them to the park to play, and I especially enjoy wrestling with them. As parents, we want to know what our children think about and what they dream about. We want to know what they like and what makes them happy. Why? It is because we love them, and they are our children.

Nevertheless, our love for our children is still limited because we are human beings. God's love, on the other hand, is not limited. The Bible tells us that God is love! It doesn't say that God has love, like Shanna and I have for our children, but that He literally is LOVE! Magnify the love that Shanna and I have for our children a thousand times over and that still doesn't come close to the way that God loves each one of us. God wants to love on us, to be with us, and for us to truly know Him. The problem is that few of us take the time to get to know Him.

We may have grown up hearing about Him in Sunday school. We may have read some of the Bible, so we are familiar with stories of Him. Still, few of us arrive at the place where we have an intimate relationship with Him. The implication is this: if we are not spending time on a daily basis getting to know Him, then we are missing out on one of the very purposes for which we were created. WE WERE MADE TO KNOW HIM!

If we are too busy to know Him, then we are missing out on the

53

very reason we were created. The better we know God, the more we experience His love. The better we know God, the more we understand what God wants and desires of us.

Good Works

■ **Ephesians 2:8, 9** "For it is by grace that you have been saved, through faith—and this not from yourselves, it is a gift from God—not by works, so that no one can boast."

We can see from this passage of Scripture, that no matter how hard we try, we cannot "work" our way into heaven. Salvation comes by grace and not by works. However, with that said, we cannot negate the fact that "works" are an important part of our Christian faith.

In Matthew 5:16, Jesus said, "In the same way, let your light shine before men, that they see your good deeds (works) and praise your Father in heaven."

55

Though our good works cannot save us, they can be that light that leads other to the foot of the cross. Our works could be the very thing that softens even the hardest of hearts. Through our good deeds, we may arouse an interest in an unbeliever to know more about what we are doing and why we are doing it. Christians never really know when they might be the only representation of Jesus Christ that another will ever see or know.

Paul reminds us in Galatians 6:10, "Let us not become weary of doing good... ."

When was the last time that you did a good deed? When was the last time that you went out of your way to serve someone? When was the last time that you gave selflessly of yourself to help another person? When people look at your life, do they see a good representation of Jesus?

Prayer

As we can see from many characters in the Bible, prayer not only gives life to the believer, but it can literally change the history of men, governments, cities, and nations.

Through the written Word, we know that Abraham prayed in his old age for a son. Even though it was naturally improbable, God answered Abraham's prayer and blessed him with a son.

Hannah prayed and begged God for a son, and God blessed her with a son who would become a powerful prophet.

Moses prayed and cried out to his Lord for victory over the Egyptians, and the Lord answered. God parted the Red Sea, allowing Moses and his people to escape from the clutches of their terrible enemy.

The prophet Elijah prayed, and it did not rain for 3½ years. Then, he prayed again, and the heavens poured out rain upon the earth.

The 120 believers were in the upper room, fasting and praying for ten days and waiting for the Promised Gift of the Father. Suddenly, the place was shaken, and they were all filled with the Holy Spirit and Power.

When Peter was sitting in a prison cell, the Church began to pray fervently for victory over the situation at hand. While Peter was still chained between two soldiers, the Lord answered the prayers of the Saints by miraculously delivering him from his chains and the guards around him.

When the sick, tormented, and demon possessed were prayed for by Jesus and His disciples, their lives were changed and they were set free from their bondages.

Man has always prayed to God, and God has always answered. He always has and always will. In fact, if He didn't, He would be a liar because in Matthew 7:7 Jesus says, "Ask and it will be given to you!" There is absolutely nothing that God cannot do if it will advance His kingdom and is in accord with His will through prayer.

Prayer releases God's power! Every revival known to mankind has been birthed from people's prayers. Every revival I have ever read about started when a group of people began to pray! Pray changes things!

If you need a miracle in your body, PRAY.
If you need a miracle in your marriage, PRAY!
If you need a better job, PRAY!
If you need a miracle in your finances, PRAY!
If you need answers or direction, PRAY!

Let's follow what Paul says in 1 Thessalonians 5:17: "Pray without ceasing."

CON DIOS LO IMPOSIBLE NO EXISTE!

How Committed Am I?
part one

■ **Each** and every one of us needs to step back, take a good look at our own lives, and ask ourselves: "How committed am I?"

How committed am I to God?
How committed am I to my family?
How committed am I to the Body of Christ?
How committed am I to bettering my community?
How committed am I to helping fulfill The Great Commission?
How committed am I to making a Godly home?
How committed am I to raising Godly children?
How committed am I to honoring God with my finances?
How committed am I to praying for my friends and loved ones?
How committed am I to living in obedience to God?
How committed am I to taking care of my body, which is the
    temple of the Holy Spirit?
How committed am I to reading God's Word?

You see, commitment is not something that is seldom talked about in our society any more. We basically live in a society without commitments. We have television shows like "Desperate Housewives" that display wives being unfaithful to their husbands. We see movie star after movie star after movie star breaking their commitments to their spouses and having affairs. Every time I read the online news, I read of another CEO or president of a business stealing or embezzling money from his company. Everyday, thousands of marriages around the world end in divorce. Everyday, thousands of Christians turn their backs on God and commit some blatant sin.

I counsel person after person that just stop paying on their debts and breaking the commitments that they made with friends, family members, and banks. In churches around the world, church members get upset with something that happened or something the pastor said. Thus, they leave the church, breaking the membership commitment they had just made a short time prior. Most people stay committed to their New Year resolution for about one month; then, they break their commitment.

I don't know about you, but I am ready for some changes to be made! I do not want to live in a society where people are continually breaking their commitments! I'm ready for God to begin to move and transform our lives and lifestyles! First, there's a question we must deal with in order to reach this point.

59

How Committed Am I?
part two

▨ **If we** want to people who are committed, we must ask: what does it look like when someone makes a commitment? Let's look at a story in David's life.

While all the other Israelite soldiers ran away, these three mighty men stood their ground and fought. Out of thousands of soldiers, only these three men stayed committed to David, the army, and to all of Israel. What would have happened if these three men wouldn't have stuck around and fought? Israel would have lost these battles. Could you imagine what was going through their minds? All of their friends were running away right in the middle of battle! All these trained, strong warriors were deserting their posts! They were turning their backs on each other and on Israel. However, three of them said "No Way! We are staying and fighting! No matter what the outcome may be, we are committed to the end!" Soldiers are trained to be tough! They are trained to fight! They are trained from day one to remain committed and faithful to one another until the end! Even with such training, all of these soldiers left and abandoned their commitment.

This reminds me a lot of our churches today. Statistics tell us that the average stay for a pastor is now 16 to 18 months. In the last decade, over 100,000 men have left the ministry.

It seems that every time the devil attacks—like the Philistines attacked the Israelites—everyone runs away! It seems that every time there's a little pressure on us as believers, we would rather take off and move to a more comfortable place instead of facing the pressure or opposition. Believers all over the world say that they want to see revival take place, but it doesn't seem like they are willing to stick around long enough and fight for it. It's very rare to find people like David's three mighty men—people that are willing to stay committed to something despite the opposition! Will you be like one of his three men or will you run away when the pressure builds?

How Committed Am I?
part three

▓ **I'm not sure** if you are aware of these facts or not, but listen to how committed Christ's early disciples were to Him.

James the son of Zebedee was beheaded.
Philip was scourged and thrown into prison only to be crucified.
Matthew was chopped into pieces.
James was stoned then beheaded in Jerusalem.
Andrew was crucified on a cross.
Mark was dragged and torn into pieces by an angry mob
    of people.
Peter was crucified up-side-down.
Paul was beheaded.
Jude was crucified.
Bartholomew was beaten then crucified.
Thomas was speared to death by pagan priests.
Luke was hung from an Olive Tree.
Simon was crucified.

These men were committed to the point of death! They literally laid down their lives for what they believed! Because they willing to do so, the Gospel continued to be spread, thousands upon thousands of people were saved, and many were healed by the power of God! That's the type of life that I want to live...a life so committed to Christ that I would take a bullet for Him...a life so committed to Christ that I would never turn my back on Him...a life so committed to Christ that I would do whatever He wanted me to do and go wherever He wanted me to go. What kind of life do you desire to live?

Under the Shadow
of the Almighty

Psalm 17:8 "Keep me as the apple of your eye; hide me in the shadow of your wings."

What would it have been like to be Adam and Eve, walking and talking with God in the Garden of Eden?

Sure, I talk to God just about every morning. I spend time daily seeking His face. Yes, believe it or not, He does talk back to me. It is not always a one-sided conversation. What would it have been like to walk with God in the Garden of Eden and literally have His shadow cast upon us? I mean if Peter's shadow could bring a physical healing to people, can you imagine what kind of experiences we could have being under the Shadow of the Almighty?

Lord, I ask that each person reading this experiences your presence in a fresh, exciting way throughout the day today and that each one of us can literally sense Your shadow being cast upon us. Amen.

Preparing for Success

In Proverbs 6, we find a few interesting facts regarding ants and how it is that these little creatures are able to survive like they do. If we took the time to review this passage of Scripture, we would see that the ants are successful because they are in constant preparation. Constant preparation is something I believe we need to implement in our lives, as well. Some time ago, I heard Pastor Scott Wilson, pastor of The Oaks Fellowship in Texas, state, "You will be tomorrow what you are planning for today!" Of course that wasn't an original quote that he trademarked or copyrighted, but it is obviously a true statement. From the moment that I first heard Scott say it, it has become one of my favorite sayings. In fact, I not only believe it, but I try to practice it in my own life. I also teach about this principle every chance I get. With that said, allow me to share with you a few thoughts on preparing for success.

1. We need to pray (John 16:13).

2. We need to observe the wind (Acts 27:13).
   —cycles, trends, culture

3. We need to be constantly evaluating (Proverbs 27:23).
   —What are people saying?
   —What is the environment around you like?
   —How are people responding to you and your leadership?
   —How are people reacting to your decisions?

4. We need to make plans (Proverbs 32:8).
   —If you aim at nothing you will hit nothing!
   —Even if you don't stick to them 100%, at least you will have a direction.

Eric Ferguson

5. We need to take responsibility.

6. We need to EXPAND our perspective and viewpoint (Acts 1:8).
   —We cannot limit God and what He wants to do.
   —We need to dream big, dream aloud, and dream in full color.
   —Get around other dreamers and out-of-the-box thinkers.

65

Renewing our Minds with the Truth
part one

Romans 12:2 "Do not conform any longer to the pattern of this world, but be transformed by the renewing of your mind. Then you will be able to test and approve what God's will is—His good, pleasing and perfect will."

How many of you want God's good, perfect, and pleasing will for your life? Well, the only way to get it is if our minds are renewed! Paul tells us to "be transformed by the renewing of your mind."

There are people that have said hurtful words to us. There are people who have acted wrongly toward us, leaving negative thoughts in our minds. Some of you have memories from our childhood that continually haunt you. As difficult as it may be, Romans tells us that we need to renew our minds. Think of it this way...we need to reprogram our minds. When our computer gets a virus and is contaminated, we often try to fix it, but sometimes we just can't. As a result, what do we do? We erase the memory and reprogram it.

Now, of course, we can't completely erase our minds, but we can reprogram them. We reprogram them with the Word of God—the Truth of God's Word! Some of us live our entire lives based completely on the lies that we believe. (You're dumb; You're good for nothing; You're stupid; You're a slut; You are worthless; You're never going to amount to anything). These are all lies from the devil that effect every decision we make. Remember, everything starts in the mind. The way we think will literally affect our destiny.

Renewing our Minds with the Truth
part two

▒ **If the way** we think directly affects our life, then instead ot buying into these lies that people have spoken over us and that we have bought into, we need to begin to proclaim God's Word!

> I am more than a conqueror through Christ Jesus!
> I am God's workmanship!
> I can do all things through Christ who strengthens me!
> I am the head and not the tail, above and not below!
> I have the mind of Christ!
> The devil is under my feet!

67

Ephesians 4:22, 23 "You were taught, with regard to your former way of life, to put off your old self, which is being corrupted by it's deceitful desires; to be made new in the attitude of your minds; and to put on the new self, created to be like God in true righteousness and holiness."

The only way we are going to have our minds made new is to get in the Word and to pray. The only way we can become more like God and to have Christ-like thinking is to align ourselves with God and His Word. We need to change the way we think, so we can change the way we act. Therefore, we must be aligned with God and His Word.

The Need For Vision
part one

■ **If you** want to be successful, you must have a vision. If you want to be productive, you must develop a vision for what you are doing and what you want to do. If you want to have a powerful ministry, you must have a vision of where you want to go. If you want to be a strong leader, you must have a vision and be a person of vision.

Napoleon saw Italy but not the Alps. He had a vision and knew where he was going. The Alps were simply something that needed to be crossed. A person with a vision of bettering his life and earning a college degree will remain steadfast until graduation. The exams, the long nights, the student loans, the odd jobs to pay the bills are simply the price that is paid in exchange for the greater reward. The majority of people will always see the obstacles that are in the path. However, truly successful people hang onto their visions and dreams and see the hope that lie beyond the obstacles.

I heard it once said that "a blind man's world is limited to the power of his touch. An ignorant man's world is limited by his knowledge. And a great man's world is limited only by his vision."

Solomon wrote in Proverbs 29:18 that "without a vision the people perish." Solomon was saying that if people do not have dreams and vision to hold onto to and to shoot for, then they will eventually die. They will have nothing to live for—nothing to motivate them. As a result, they will eventually loose that drive to thrive. If you want to have fruitful ministry, if you want to develop your cell groups, churches, and leadership, begin to visualize what success is for you. It is imperative that each one of us has a vision. We must have that ultimate goal for which we are living.

The Need For Vision
part two

There is a Charlie Brown cartoon (the one that Dr. John Maxwell often uses as an illustration) that shows Charlie Brown in the back yard shooting arrows at his fence. After he shot all the arrows in the fence, he walked over and drew a huge circle around all the arrows. Lucy happened to see Charlie Brown doing this, so she told him that he wasn't shooting the bow and arrows properly...that he needed to have a target at which to shoot. Charlie Brown, however, insisted that his way was right and told Lucy that with his way he never missed! Charlie Brown makes a good point: If you aim at nothing, you will hit nothing.

Thus, we must have an aim—a vision. When you keep your vision in front of you, you can grow a church to 1,000 or 5,000 or even 10,000. You can develop 100 cell groups in your ministry area. You can reach 3,000 children in the children's ministry, and you can send 10 young people to Bible college to become ministers.

Vision helps determine where you are headed. It's like one of my favorite illustrations that I like to share. You wouldn't try to put a 10,000 piece puzzle together without first looking at the picture on the box. However, that's exactly what many of us do in life and ministry. We don't step back, take a good look at the big picture, and develop a vision of where we want to go. Instead, we just move full steam ahead, many times without any real direction and purpose. We start a new church or ministry because we feel that's what we should do, but we never have a vision of what we want this new church or ministry to become. Unfortunately, many people fall flat of their faces but can't figure out why.

It is vision that helps us determine where we are going...AND MORE IMPORTANTLY, why we are even there in the first place!

The Principle
of Promotion
part one

At one point of being the senior executive pastor of a church, I had an assistant who was in his early 20s and who formerly worked at a bank. Listen to how God works in the lives of His children. In less than a year of working at the bank, my assistant was promoted and began to work directly with the General Manager. Then, shortly afterward, he was given the permission to prepare documents and statements for the General Manager of the bank. How could a young man obtain such a position at bank? It is due to the Principle of Promotion!

God gives favor and promotion to those that seek first His Kingdom and His righteousness (Matthew 6:33).

In Luke 14:11, Jesus said, "For everyone who exalts himself will be humbled, and he who humbles himself will be exalted."

In the Kingdom of God, promotion comes by humility.

In Matthew 18, the disciples of Jesus wanted to know who was the greatest in the Kingdom of God. In response, Jesus set a little child in front of all the people to see. Jesus did not call the most popular person, the wisest person, the richest person, or the most experienced person as an example. Jesus put a simple, little child in front of them and said that they needed to become like on of them! Jesus taught clearly that whoever humbles himself like a little child shall be the greatest in the Kingdom of God.

When I think of a humble person who is seeking first the Kingdom of God, I think of my brother-in-law Pastor Jeff Leake. He became the senior pastor of the Allison Park Church when he was around 23 years old. Before he became the senior pastor, Jeff was serving as the associate pastor, but during that time, the senior pastor resigned. Thus, the board began to look for a new senior pastor and decided that Jeff would be a great candidate. Even though the board wanted him and the congregation wanted him, in his humility, he originally declined the offer. However, after much prayer and thought, he eventually did accept the position as senior pastor. Over the next few years, Jeff implemented a very aggressive church planting strategy, and in a six-year time frame, he planted five churches. However, during this entire time period, he never once promoted himself, his ideas, or his success. Instead, Jeff continued seeking God first and believing in Him for bigger and better things to come. Shortly after the church's success with the church plants, different churches in the United States were calling Jeff and offering him the position of senior pastor over thousands of people. Jeff continually declined. Then, he started receiving invitations to speak at conferences and huge events. All of the sudden, Jeff became a very popular conference speaker on the subject of church planting.

Why did these promotions happen?

Pastor Jeff was promoted because he continually sought after the Kingdom of God and His righteousness first and remained humble before the Lord. As a child of God, he began to receive the promises of God and began to experience the Principle of Promotion in his life.

The Principle of Promotion
part two

■ **In the Bible**, we can see example after example of people who received promotions from the Lord.

David was just a small shepherd boy but became king.
Joseph was sold into slavery but became the 2nd in command of the entire region.
Esther was just a little virgin girl, but she became a queen.
Peter was a common fisherman, but God used him as a foundation to build the church.

As followers of Christ, God wants us to experience this Principle of Promotion. The promises of God, the provision of God, and the promotion of God are things that God has in store for us. However, many of us will never experience all that God has planned for us because we are not doing what Jesus said in Matthew 6: "SEEK FIRST THE KINGDOM OF GOD, and HIS RIGHTEOUSNESS!"

Unfortunately, many people compromise and are not totally committed to the Kingdom of God. They want the promises of God to come to pass in their lives. They want to experience the provisions of God in their lives. They want to receive the promotions of God in their lives. However, they are unwilling to fully commit to God and to seek first His Kingdom! Thus, they live frustrated lives because they know the truth and they know what they should do, but they are still trying to serve two kingdoms.

God doesn't want us to compromise. He wants us to be totally committed to pursuing His Kingdom. Jesus said that for those that leave everything for His sake, God will reward them 100 times more in this life and the life to come. We must get to the point in our lives where we do not pursue things that will hinder our pursuit of God's Kingdom. If there are certain things in our lives that are a temptation to us, we need to avoid them. If we are attracted to or drawn toward a particular thing that we know will cause us to fall, we need to remain far from it. If we know that we are tempted when we are around certain people, we need to stay away from them. It's that plain and simple. We need to use our common sense on some of these things. WE NEED TO BE 100% COMMITTED TO THE KINGDOM OF GOD! WE NEED TO PURSUE RIGHTEOUSNESS! AS CHRISTIANS, THERE IS NO OTHER PURSUIT FOR US—JUST THE THINGS OF GOD!

We live in a world where there are two Kingdoms at conflict—the Kingdom of Darkness versus the Kingdom of God. This Kingdom conflict will continue to exist until Jesus Christ returns the earth to defeat Satan once and for all. However, until that happens, the key for us is to choose the Kingdom of God and to let go of the Kingdom of Darkness.

No compromise!

Make a stand!

Pursue righteousness, holiness, and the Truth!

Refining and Maturing

James 1:2-5 "Consider it pure joy, my brothers, whenever you face trials of many kids, because the testing of your faith develops perseverance. Perseverance must finish its work so that you may be mature and complete, not lacking anything."

I'm not one to believe that God sends bad things our way to mature us, but I do believe that He allows us to go through things in order to teach us things and mature us. In the above Scripture, James was writing to the early Christian believers who were dispersed right after the stoning of Stephen. The Christians were being persecuted and chased out of their towns, so James writes to them and tells them that they should consider it joy to be facing the things that they were facing. Now, of course, James wasn't saying that they should be joyful because they were being persecuted, but he said they should consider it a joy. James understood that if his fellow believers could endure the hardships, they would become much stronger, more mature people.

1 Peter 1:6-7 "In this you greatly rejoice, though now for a little while you may have had to suffer grief in all kinds of trials. These have come so that your faith—of greater worth than gold, which perishes even though refined by fire—may be proved genuine and may result in praise, glory and honor when Jesus Christ is revealed."

Also, consider what Paul wrote to the believers at Corinth.
2 Corinthians 4:16, 17 "Therefore we do not lose heart. Though outwardly we are wasting away, yet inwardly we are being renewed day by day. For our light and momentary troubles are achieving for us an eternal glory that far outweighs them all."

The trials and troubles in our lives act like the way weights affect muscles. When you lift weights, your muscles begin to grow. The more weights and resistance you put on the muscle, the bigger and more developed it gets. If the muscle isn't trained, it will never develop to its full potential.

It's the same way with our lives. If we never go through trials, we will never grow to our full capacity. If we are never challenged by obstacle and hardships, we will never know who we really are and of what we are made. James tells us that it is when we are tested that we actually grow and develop. When the pressure is on us, it is then that we can see what is really inside of us. Then, we can take those things to the Lord and allow Him to work in us.

I tell you what, with all the stress and trials that I have allowed to take my peace over the last few years, I have had the opportunity to see parts of me that I do not like. I discovered attitudes that I had to take to the Lord and allow Him to work on.

Thus, I really like this Chinese Proverb: "The gem cannot be polished without friction, nor man perfected without trials!"

James said to "consider it pure joy, my brothers, whenever you face trials of many kinds" because he knew that they were going to experience trials in their lives. We all do and all will. Trials and challenges are part of life. The key, though, is how we react to those things. If, like James says, we keep a good attitude and allow God to do something in our lives during our season of trials, then we will come out victorious and a more mature person.

However, if we get a bad attitude and turn hard and bitter because of life's hardships, then we won't have the victory that God wants us to have and will not mature in the things of the Lord. I once heard it said that "if life throws you a lemon, make lemonade!" It is our choice. Sure, it is hard to accept and deal with some of the things we have to go through in life, but knowing that God is with us, is working on our behalf and wants to do something in our lives as we pass through "the fire," we can still have peace!

The Needs of the Bride
part one

Believers are the Bride of Christ. Several places in the Scriptures it mentions that the Bride must prepare herself for the wedding banquet or Christ's return. Our responsibility as pastors is to help prepare the Bride for Christ's second coming. Part of preparing the Bride for Christ's return is to treat the bride properly. As pastors, we often forget to treat the Bride of Christ the way that Christ would want us to. We often get frustrated with the Bride and don't respect her the way that we should. Often times, the Bride doesn't treat us well; so in turn, we respond with words or actions that don't please God. However, this is not correct.

For example, Shanna is my Bride—my beautiful wife and the love of my life! It is my job as her husband to treat her well and take care of her. I made a covenant agreement with her to always love her…for better and for worse and in sickness and in health. In this same way, we should love the Bride of Christ. Over the next few days, let us consider four things that we need to provide of the Bride of Christ. We will look at the first one today.

"Be shepherds of God's flock that is under your care, serving as overseers—not because you must, but because you are willing, as God wants you to be; not greedy for money, but eager to serve; not lording it over those entrusted to you, but being examples to the flock. And when the Chief Shepherd appears, you will receive the crown of glory that will never fade away."

We are shepherds, and the Bride is our flock. As pastors who are responsible for caring for the Bride, we must feed her. When we feed her, we are called to do so willingly and eagerly. When our attitude is pleasing to God, we will be positive examples to the Bride of how she should go to others in the Bride and do likewise.

"I gave you milk, not solid food, for you were not yet ready for it. Indeed, you are still not ready."

Through this statement of Paul, it is evident that there comes a time in the Bride's life that she needs to receive solid food. Just like my wife needs a well-balanced diet in order to live life to the fullest and to be in good health, the Bride of Christ needs to receive a well-balanced diet of teaching and preaching. She needs a good balance of the entire Bible— Old Testament and New Testament. Too much of one thing will cause an imbalance. Prosperity Message, Faith Movement, Healing Ministries, River Movements, Gold Fillings, Holy Laughter—these things all have a place in the Body of Christ, but they cannot be our only focus. It is our responsibility to give the Bride a solid, well-balanced diet.

The Needs of the Bride
part two

■ **The Bride** of Christ needs protection.

It is my responsibility to protect my wife. When we walk down the street, I am supposed to walk closest to the street in order to protect her from being hit and/or splashed by cars. As we leave a restaurant or movie and it's late in the evening, Shanna cuddles up under my arm while we are walking through the dark parking lot. Why? It is because she wants me to protect her, and she wants to feel safe.

Psalm 5:11 "But let all who take refuge in you be glad; let them ever sing for joy. Spread your protection over them that those who love your name may rejoice in you."

1 Corinthians 13:7 "[Love] always protects, always trusts, always hopes, always perseveres."

The nature of love...the nature of God...is to protect, and our nature as pastors needs to the same.

John 17:12 "While I was with them, I protected them and kept them safe by that name you gave me. None has been lost except the one doomed to destruction so that Scripture would be fulfilled."

Christ set the example for us to follow. This verse from John 17 is a part of a prayer that Jesus prayed shortly before He was arrested and crucified. He had been with His disciples for three years, and He tells the Father that He has kept His disciples safe from destruction. The only one lost was Judas—"the one doomed to destructions so that Scripture would be fulfilled."

The Needs of the Bride
part three

■ **The Bride** of Christ needs comfort.

There are times in our lives that we just need to be comforted. There are times that we just need to know that everything is going to be okay and that we have someone there that we can rely on and trust. As pastors, we need to provide such comfort to the Bride and be present for her in hard times.

2 Corinthians 1:3-5 "Praise be to the God and Father of our Lord Jesus Christ, the Father of compassion and the God of all comfort, who comforts us in all our troubles, so that we can comfort those in any trouble with the comfort we ourselves have received from God. For just as the sufferings of Christ flow over into our lives, so also through Christ our comfort overflows."

God comforts us so that we can comfort the Bride. If we aren't comforted, we need to draw closer to God for ourselves.

Colossians 4:11 "Jesus, who is called Justus, also sends greetings. These are the only Jews among my fellow workers for the kingdom of God, and they have proved a comfort to me."

Paul wrote the epistle of Colossians from prison, and he writes in the last chapter that his fellow workers for the kingdom of God have comforted him."

2 Corinthians 7:6-7 "But God, who comforts the downcast, comforted us by the coming of Titus, and not only by his coming but also by the comfort you had given him."

Clearly, God uses people to give His comfort to the Bride. He used Titus, and He wants to use you too! There are too many among His Bride hurting and in distress, so allow yourself to be a vessel through which His comfort flows.

The Needs of the Bride
part four

■ **The Bride** of Christ needs exhortation.

My wife needs exhortation. She needs encouragement. She needs to hear that she did a good job cooking dinner. She needs to know that I really appreciate her taking care of the kids. She needs to know that I'm grateful for her choosing to be my wife.

Unfortunately, we all have the tendencies to take people and things for granted. Many times, our congregations are doing such a great job carrying out the vision we have cast before them, but they never hear our affirmation. We are naturally inclined to focus on the negative instead of the positive. Instead of encouraging the Bride and exhorting her, we tear her down and destroy her. Often times, we shoot our wounded instead of helping them recover and live victoriously.

1 Thessalonians 5:12 "Now we ask you, brothers, to respect those who work hard among you, who are over you in the Lord and who admonish you."

1 Peter 2:12 "Live such good lives among the pagans that, though they accuse you of doing wrong, they may see your good deeds and glorify God on the day he visits us."

Romans 12:6-8 "We have different gifts...if it is encouraging, let him encourage; if it is contributing to the needs of others, let him give generously; if it is leadership, let him govern diligently; if it is showing mercy, let him do it cheerfully."

Hebrews 3:13 "But encourage one another daily, as long as it is called Today, so that none of you may be hardened by sin's deceitfulness."

If the Bride is not being encouraged as she lives for her Bridegroom—Jesus Christ—then it will be easier for her to be "hardened by sin's deceitfulness."

Hebrews 10:25 "Let us not give up meeting together, as some are in the habit of doing, but let us encourage one another—and all the more as you see the Day approaching."

Every time our congregations meet for services, the atmosphere needs to be charged with encouragement. These days, encouragement is seldom found on the streets, in the workplace, or in schools. Thus, the church must be a place of encouragement for the Bride!

81

The Origin of Sin

James 1:13-15 "When tempted, no one should say that God is tempting me. For God cannot be tempted by evil, nor does He tempt anyone, but each one is tempted when, by his own evil desire, he is dragged away and enticed. Then, after desire has conceived, it gives birth to sin, and sin, when it is full-grown, gives birth to death."

Where does Sin come from?

Many people seem to think that God is the originator of sin. They think He sits up in heaven and puts things in our paths that would cause us to stumble or sin. However, God is not and cannot be the author or creator of sin. ALL sin must be traced back to Adam and Eve and their rebellion against God. Because of their mistake, we are all born with a sinful nature—a nature that lends us to giving into the desires of our flesh.

Does sin grow?

According to James, sin does grow, or maybe I should say, it "progresses" in our lives. Think about the life of a child for a moment. When children are two or three years old, they are already beginning to lie and maybe even steal things like cookies and candy. However, over the next few years, they often progress into deceiving, cheating, cussing, fits of rage, etc. Without the knowledge of Christ, sin progresses very quickly in our lives.

Where does sin take us?

Sin separates us from God. By definition of sin itself, sin is the separation from God. Therefore, if people never deal with the fact that they are sinners, they will ultimately be separated from God forever. James tell us that sin leads to DEATH. Death, or an eternal separation from God, is the penalty for our sins.

Romans 1:18 "The wrath of God is being revealed from heaven against all the godless and wickedness of men."

Romans 6:23 "For the wages of sin is DEATH…"

I thank God that Paul goes on to tell us in Romans 6:23 that "the wages of sin is DEATH, but the GIFT of God is eternal life in Christ Jesus our Lord!"

CPSIA information can be obtained at www.ICGtesting.com
Printed in the USA
LVOW082247040512

280375LV00001B/9/P